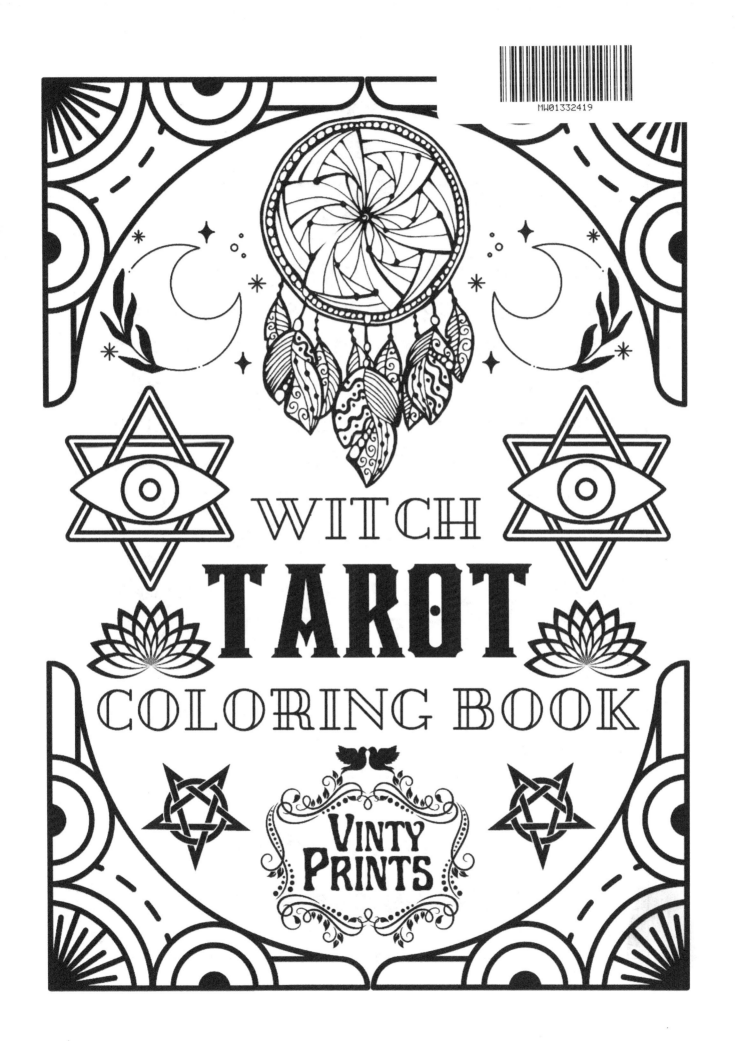

Behind each main coloring page there is a bleed page which is intended to protect your work from bleed through. For complete protection from bleed through, it is recommended to place a piece of card behind the page you are working on, particularly if you are using strong inks.

On each bleed sheet, you will find a variation of tarot affirmations, positive quotes and magical illustrations.

Happy Coloring!

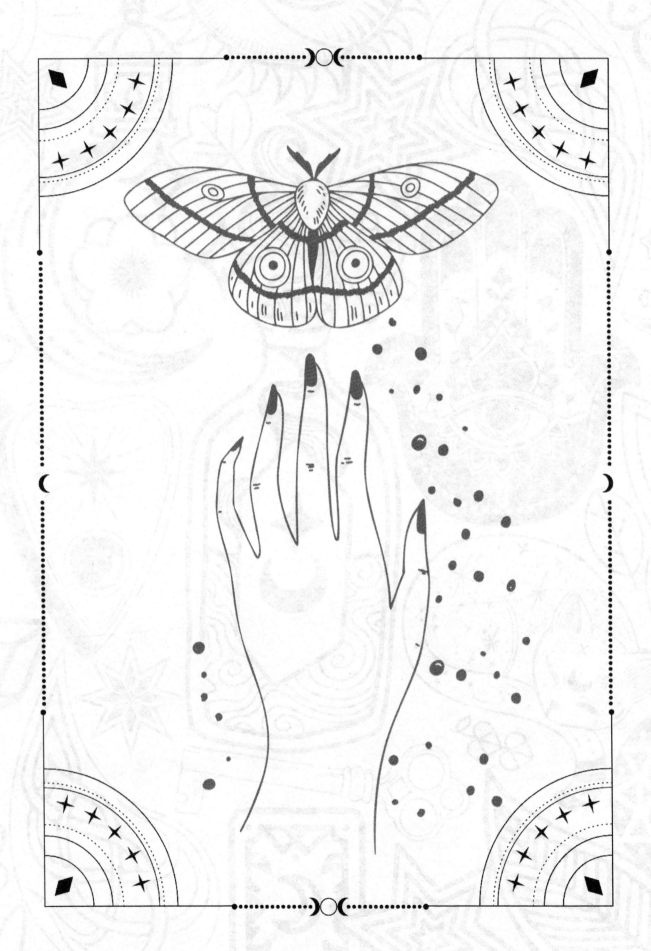

You have the power to make changes and feel complete.

Never lose hope. When the sun goes down, the stars come out.

Happiness is not a matter of intensity but of balance, order, rhythm and harmony.

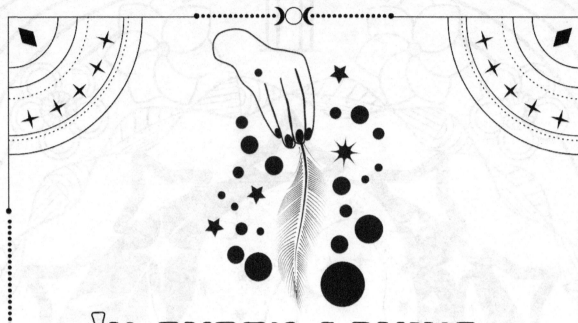

In every loving woman there is a priestess of the past

The devil whispered in my ear "You're not strong enough to withstand the storm" Today I whispered in the devil's ear

"I AM THE STORM"

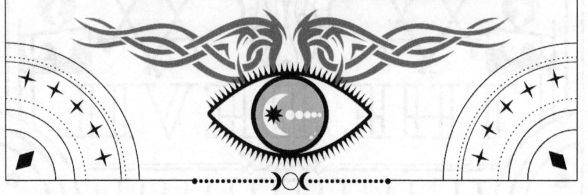

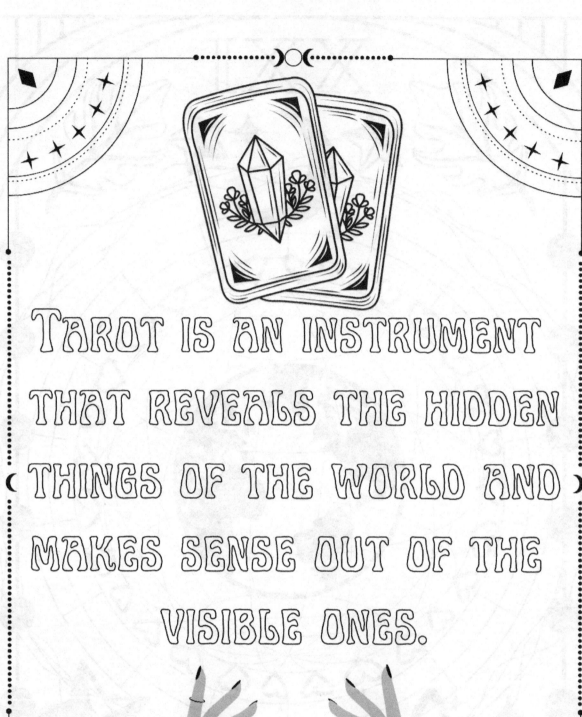

Tarot is an instrument that reveals the hidden things of the world and makes sense out of the visible ones.

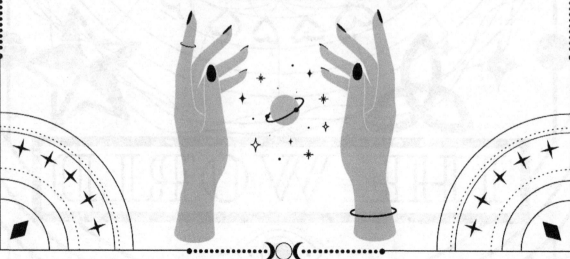

In order to own the light within, we must be willing to explore the shadow.

The Earth is the mother of all people, and all people should have equal rights upon it.

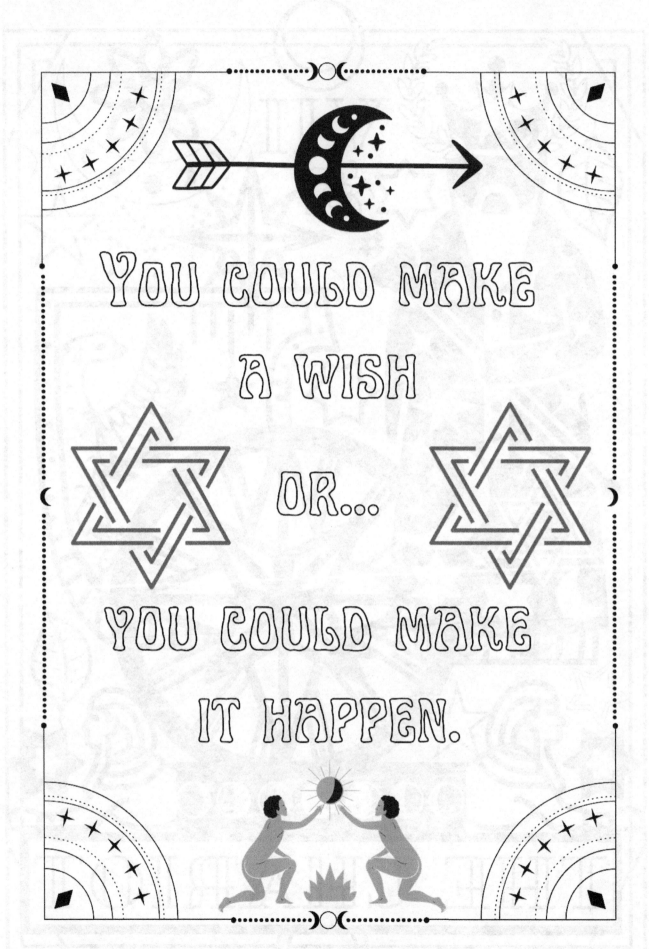

You could make a wish

or...

You could make it happen.

TAROT MAGIC

Chaos and crumbling often precede finding peace.

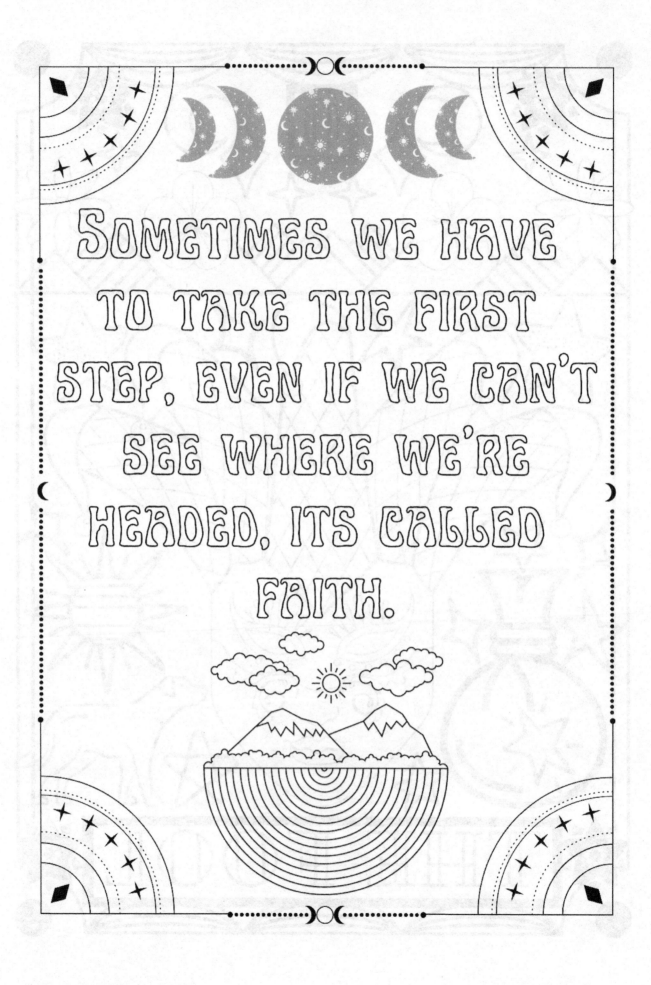

The Emperor reminds us that we all have the power to rule our own lives.

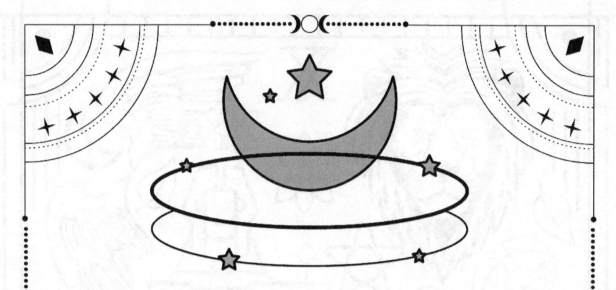

Blessed are those who believe without seeing.

Hang on in there. It is astonishing how short a time it can take for very wonderful things to happen.

Tarot is an incredible, powerful tool for spiritual development, personal insight, transformation and change.

Those of us who connect and walk with the ancients are drawn to days of the old, we feel the stars and the moon deep within our bones, a bond formed during creation.

Hope you loved this tarot coloring book Thank You

Made in the USA
Monee, IL
14 September 2025